D1297171

PONY

Tony Curtis & David Lilburn

PONY

Tony Curtis & David Lilburn

Occasional Press

Contents

Images

"Good God, what a land of breeders, you see quadrupeds everywhere."

Molloy by Samuel Beckett

Pony

The Lord of dust and darkness
      Is the Pit Pony –
Who would take his place below?

The Lord of icy winds and bare islands
      Is the Shetland Pony –
Who would stand all night in the rain with her?

The Lord of bog, mountain, lakes, rivers
      Is the Connemara Pony –
Who would disappear into mist with one?

Two Poems
After my first visit to a pony show in Clifden

On Getting Advice from Sean Halpenny

I asked the man holding the reins
How much he wanted for his horse,

But he just looked out across the hills
As if considering the sweetness of grass.

Under his cap he had the face of a bird
Sheltering out of the rain.

When I asked Sean
Why the man ignored me,

He said, "You called his pony
A horse. That is like calling

A bodhrán
A drum,

A currach
A boat.

It's a wonder he didn't smack you;
I would have."

In Foyle's Hotel, Clifden

"And do you like ponies, Martin?"
"Ay! I do, but not enough to ride one.

They are not like cows or sheep.
A pony is for life, and you have

To feed them when they are old,
And they are old a long time –

Unless you butcher them. And it's hard
To butcher something with a name like Molly."

After Seven Photographic Portraits
of a Grey Connemara Pony

You will know a pony by its ears:
  Listening out for weather forecasts and love songs.

By its mane:
  Tossed over its eyes like a witch's broom.

By its coat:
  Always buttoned up, tight-fitting, dusty and well-worn.

By its eyes:
  That look at you, then look at you again to take you in.

By its hooves:
  Made for dancing, and so are worn at the tips.

By its mouth:
  That loves to eat words given with pats of the hand.

By its nose:
  That knows you, and lifts the pony's head to let it know you're coming.

By its tail:
  That conducts the symphony of birdsong, lake-song, light-song
  That is the bog underfoot, here above the village of Roundstone.

Old Books and Riverbanks

I asked Dan Magee
What he thought
Ponies smelt of.
"Piss and grass," he said,

"Though if my mother asked me,
I'd say a small bird's nest
After the eggs have hatched
And the birds have flown."

I asked his wife the same question.
She said, "Dan's breath after
A plate of grilled kidneys –
A slight urine tinge on the tongue."

"Although," she added, "in summer
A pony can smell of hay,
Wild strawberries,
Honey and hedgerows,

Or a crumpled featherbed
Abandoned by lovers,
Or the feather pillows
Where their heads lay."

I asked an old woman
Who keeps Connemara ponies
Out there somewhere
Along the Errislannan Road

What they smell like?
She worded
And wondered.
"Old churches," she said,

"Like the creaky 'Star of the Sea'
That faces into the wind at Omey.
Go inside," she said,
"Sure, it's always open,

Close your eyes,
Breathe in,
And it is like you're
Standing beside a pony.

Blessed creatures. Faithful.
Sure, didn't Jesus himself
Ride one all over the Holy Land.
Do you know your Bible at all?"

When her granddaughter,
Amelia, joined us, I asked
 Her what ponies smelt of.
"Dust," she said, "fairy dust."

Then I asked a small boy.
He said, "The men's toilet
After the big match:
Guinness, farts and wet grass."

And me? I think ponies
Smell of old books, riverbanks,
Bogs, and wool just washed
And hung out in the wind to dry.

Where Do I Go to Find a Connemara Pony?

You follow the light west
    Until trees and grass
        Give way to bare hills,
            Lakes, streams and bogs.

And then, when the lane gives out
    By the edge of the sea –
        Well, you are almost there –
            Follow the waves along the beach,

On and on to where the cliffs,
    The rocks and the water
        Are too high or too deep to carry on,
            To go even another step forward.

Now stand there a while,
    Listening to the salt wind
        Until they appear up out of the earth
            Moving towards you like grey, misty ghosts.

The old folk will tell you that ponies still go back
    And forth between here and Tír na nÓg.
        But you'll never discover the way.
            You see, you don't find the ponies, they find you.

Pony Time

Ponies don't have days of the week;
They judge things by the light.
If it is sunny and bright, it's a Saturday:
They can lie in, sleep late on the grass,
Swim or stand by the shore.
If it is grey, raining, and everything
Is covered in mist, then it's a Monday:
They hunker down and just get through.

Connemara Rain

The Connemara grey pony
Is the same faithful colour
As Connemara rain.

Some morning go out
Onto the turf-tumbling bog,
Bring your pony.

Stand by a wall,
One of those made of stones
Balanced on hope.

When the rain begins,
Hold the reins tightly,
Look into its eyes.

Then as the rain falls,
Watch the pony slowly vanish
Before your eyes.

It's a sort of rainy miracle,
But out on the bog
It happens every wet day.

I can't be certain,
But I think Connemara rain
And Connemara ponies

Are related to clouds,
Mist, frost,
Snowflakes and mirrors.

Mirrors and the soft faces of lakes.

Two Poems:
From the Roundstone Pony Show

Dam
To the tune of "Saddle The Pony"
              for old Irish flute.

The way he taps her white bottom with the whip –
Softly, slowly – you just know he loves her.

"That's the girl," he mutters, "that's the girl.
Easy, easy and slow now. Easy and slow."

His words falling over and into
Her white ears like ghost whispers.

Sire
The Colt and the Poet

His body is a temple
Where all is worked on,
Worked over, supple and oiled.

My body is a shed
Where everything is damp,
Stiff, cobwebbed and rusting.

The Pony Races on Omey Island

Omey,
Oh my!

I put it all on a pony
At the sand races on Omey:

The house, the farm, the money.
If only it had won, if only.

It was fast but ran the wrong way,
The wrong direction entirely;

Off towards the clouds of grey
Gathering on the hills far away.

When he finds out, he'll surely kill me
And bury me with that pony on Omey.

Omey,
Oh my!

The Bad Breeder

I.

In his cap, coat and brown trousers
He looks like a breeder

Ought to; the old grey
Fellow holding the pony.

Though he looks
Like he has only half his wits,

He would best and hurl
You in a pony deal.

You would be like horse
Manure in his hands.

Still, he'd spit on your collar
To make you softer.

I heard one buyer mutter,
after a deal that turned to disaster,

"That man's promises
curdle on his lips.

His ponies are too tall or too small.
Best not to breed with them at all.

I hope his wife makes hay with a priest,
And his daughter marries a ghost.

A pox on all his breed
And all his seed."

II.

Another man points at the breeder
Saying, "He's only a chancer.

Wasn't I a stupid dunce?
Didn't I buy a pony off him once?

It looked good: nice coat, clear eyes,
But one icy wind and it passed away.

Sure, that wasn't a pony at all,
That was a different class of animal,

Something related to camel or duck.
Wasn't I the fool to trust to luck?

And look! Look how calm
The pony is in his hands. Pure calm.

That's what fooled me.
That's what fooled me entirely.

And his wife, she's just the same.
In fact, she's even better at the game.

She softens you with womanly guile,
Empties your pockets with her smile.

A pox on their breed
And on their seed."

The Pony's Eyes

You see the bog
In greens and browns.

Ponies see it
In yellows and whites.

If ponies could paint,
The sky would be silver,

The sea a vivid red,
The islands blue.

Lakes would be golden.
Blackbirds would be yellow.

Think on it,
Then wonder no more

Why ponies always
Stand there looking amazed.

The School Desk

It was the old school desk
Where I was taught
To string words together
By a man with a stammer,
A Bible, a black stick, and the
Connemara pony he called Cicero.
I used to call him Banjo.

He liked to quote Shakespeare
And read us the poetry of John
Clare and Patrick Kavanagh –
The two angels at his table.
A good man, he had a face like rain.
Some days he was all grief like
A scarecrow. He'd shake his stick at us
As if we were a flock of crows.

He married a woman from Maam Cross.
They had eleven boys
Named after the apostles.
I was good friends with Thaddaeus
And Bartholomew. I still wonder -
If they'd had a twelfth child,
Would they have dared to call him Judas?

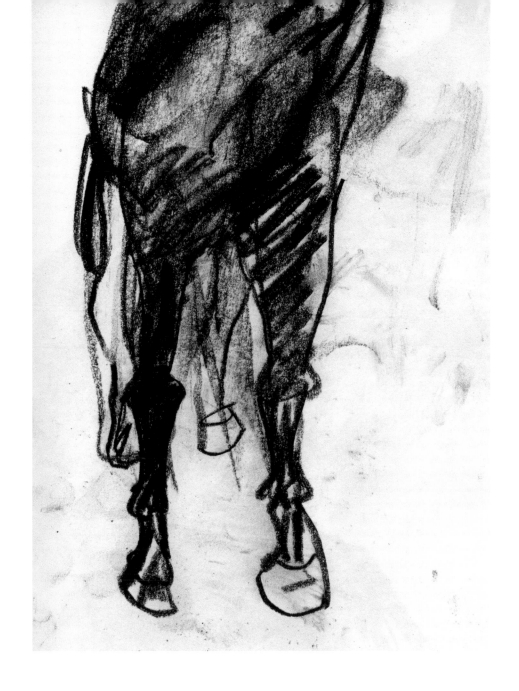

34

Did You Ever Scream at a Pony?

I did, just the once, on the Errislannan Road –
That's way out west in Connemara –
I was coming back from Brendan's house
After a night on the whiskey and beer.
I was all bendy like an accordion,
Floating along like a feather in the dark,
Singing *The Rocky Road To Dublin*.
It was a night so black, so absolutely still,
I could have been in the grave.
Suddenly, a creature whinnied in my ear.
Every ghost and bog goblin that wandered the roads
Appeared before me in a moment of pure terror.
I screamed, and the darkness swallowed
Him in a terrified drumming of hooves.

Lucian Freud on Painting a Pony

In two thousand and three, Lucian Freud
Took to painting a white pony
At a small stables in the west of London.

He said, "Painting the pony's body was
Like painting a nude, but painting the pony's
White head was like painting a portrait."

Freud is known for the years he takes over a new work.
Like his grandfather, he excavates every wrinkle
And fold to see what lies invisible on the surface.

Yet painting the pony's head took
Only twenty sessions. He said,
"Suddenly, it was quite definitely finished."

I have seen his painting of the pony's white head.
It is magnificent. He captures, perfectly,
The stillness of a bright summer morning in Connemara.

Waiting in the Rain

I sometimes see two old ponies
Out on the bog road in winter.
As I pass them, they remind me
Of the two dishevelled characters
In Samuel Beckett's play
Waiting for Godot.

It's the way their bog-brown eyes
Look at me as I carry on down the road:
A terrible, disappointed gaze –
You are not the man with the hay.
But he's coming soon, very soon.
Perhaps tomorrow.

A Frosty Night in the Stables
The Winter Solstice

I spent last night in the stables talking to a pony.
She didn't say much, but she was a great listener.
Sometimes she neighed or whinnied at what I said.
Mostly she just spoke with her bog-brown eyes,
Two pools of wisdom stolen from the harsh out there.

When all the winter light was gone from the Western sky,
We just lay there in the warm hay enjoying the peace.
I was going to read her a poem but thought better of it.
Instead I sang a couple of lines from Bob Dylan

> *All the tired horses in the sun*
> *How am I supposed to get any riding done?*

> *All the tired horses in the sun*
> *How am I supposed to get any riding done?*

Over and over until she was almost asleep, and I was ready to go.

The Artist on the Bog
for Donald Teskey

For nearly five weeks
The artist has been drawing wild
Grasses, turf ridges, walls and ruins -
All kinds of abandoned things.

Lark has begun to wonder
If he is ever going home.
She has asked the badger
And the grey pony about him,

But they just tell her
Not to worry. They say,
"Think of him as a scarecrow,
But without the straw.

He is engrossed in drawing
And painting the distance.
He is not interested in shooting
Or capturing a small bird.

He may draw you,
But he won't hurt you.
Think of him as a fence post.
In fact, sit on him."

The Herd

Ponies like to read books
On art, poetry, philosophy,
The Beats and the Irish Renaissance.
They have a liking for the early
Poems of W. B.Yeats and the later
Paintings of his brother, Jack.
They especially like the ghostly
White pony in his painting *For the Road.*
Sadly, they can't get from where
They are, way out on the bog, to look
At it in the National Gallery in Dublin.

And Pony Town? Well, you can't
Get there from where you are, either.
Winter and summer it moves with the herd.
When one grassy place is played out,
They pack up their tents, their lamps,
Their hay, their shoes, their brushes,
Their chairs, their books, their glasses,
Their ink, their pens and their paper,
And move on to where the bog grass,
The herbs and seaweed are all untrodden,
Touched only by sea-wind and salt-rain.

There they begin all over again:
Reading and telling stories,
Always adding to the old.
It is their way of life:
Generations in the making,
Uninterrupted until now.
These Connemara Ponies are as old
As the mountains, the rivers and the bogs.
Everything about them says, *Once upon a time …*
In fact, I believe they are as old as stars
Whose mark they carry on their forehead.

From the Teaching of Po-Nee
After the 17th Century Japanese

Matsuo Bashō liked to travel by pony, though mostly he walked from town to town. Po-Nee, named for his way with ponies, never travelled far from his mountain home. Unlike Bashō, he never complained about the rain, he thought of it as a heavenly blessing. He liked things green. In his small thatched room he wrote his haiku in pine charcoal. It is said he preferred herons and ponies to people. Still, he was married three times. Though his haiku and calligraphy are beautiful, unlike Bashō and Yosa Buson, he is mostly forgotten.

The Connemara Versions
for Paula Meehan

Pilgrim

So, look behind you.
Horseman, poet, monk – all dead.
Still they speak to you.

Sea

Live by the sea's edge,
Learn from the tide, wave by wave.
Be an island, float.

Shelter

On cold winter days,
Let the clouds rest on your back;
Their feathers warm you.

Rain

When the rain comes on,
Be the fool dancing for joy –
Say it's God's blessing.

Rest

Shelter in the trees,
Let birds sing sweetly to you
As if in your grave.

Light

Painter painting sky
Adds the white of a pony –
And the sun shines through.

Reader

Learn joy from the frog.
Take song and prayer from the hare.
Read the pony's book.

Ode

Like a young poet,
Say everything you have to –
Let your old soul speak.

Heritage

Live light as a leaf.
Let trees be a gathering.
At the end, let go.

Life

Let grass be your sign,
Not bright sun, white moon or stars –
Be like the wind, sway.

Prayer

When drawn to ring bells,
Fuchsia, cowslip and eyebright.
Be one with the earth.

Surrender

One hell of a night:
Though we warmed and sheltered it,
The foal passed away.

The Map

Each cloud is a map,
Each deep lake a love letter,
Each pony a poem.

The Way

If the road leads on
From dull town towards dull field –
Change, don't follow hooves.

Adapt

Look at the snow goose.
It imitates the snow flake,
Melts away in summer.

To Their Will

Po-Nee means the foal,
That which melts the eye and heart.
Yet is broken, whipped.

Wild Flowers

White-petaled flowers
Grow on the back of the bog –
White-petaled ponies.

Struggle

A day full of grief.
That said, even years from now,
Love will have no cure.

Heaven

Oats, nothing but oats;
Just a handful of barley
And straw on the floor.

Po-Nee Talks About Sahoko's Portrait
of his Eldest Daughter Momoko
After the Japanese, 17th Century

You will never really understand painters.
They have a very odd way of looking.
Take this portrait Sahoko made
Of my eldest daughter Momoko:

She painted her from the back,
Naked, with her hair tied up,
Walking into the ocean
At the midpoint of summer.
It is long after midnight,
But a full moon, full of light,
Is keeping the darkness at bay.
She is up to her shivering waist in water.
The long curve of her back
Is a pale white, silky
As a pony in moonlight.

The Tao of Grass

Ponies pray to the earth.
Morning and evening
They bow their heads
To the grass.

Like Cistercian monks,
Theirs is a silent order.
Occasionally, a prayer will
Whinny up like plain chant.

Of course
The small birds know
The ponies' prayers
Intimately.

I have seen a wren
Standing on the back of a pony
Sing a song so sweet
I know it is beyond him.

It is a tune stolen
From the ponies' prayers.
Just a fragment.
What this little bird remembers.

I can only imagine
The pool of song
From where
This melody comes.

Still Life With Pony

You could paint it yourself:

A white cottage is sunk into the mountain.
A river is falling to the sea. There are two otters
At play and a grey heron watching,
Waiting for foolish salmon, lost in
River thoughts, to swim into its gaze.
Then there's the bog: a splash of greens and browns.
The dome of the sky, a kettle grey. And under it,

A Connemara pony standing down by the shore
As if waiting for a spell to magic it back through
The rolling waves, back to the place its fathers came from.
I often wonder what calamity, what sudden happening
Made their Prince, their rider, put down his wand
And walk back into the mist without them.

On Connemara Ponies

Because they read the wind
Because they study mist
Because they would stand all night in the rain for you
Because they never complain how long the road is
Because they whinny in the dark
Because they are mistaken for ghosts
Because they follow drunks home
Because they are related to herons
Because they are made in the image of Pegasus
Because their father was Poseidon
Because where their hooves touch, water springs
Because they kiss the lake's cold lips
Because they bow down to the grass
Because they are often lonely like owls and moles
Because they talk with their eyes
Because they dance with each other like waves and blackbirds
Because they are inexhaustible as the stones of Connemara
Because their eyes say, look at these! And these! And these!
Because they stare down bog reed, bog asphodel, bog myrtle
Because they wink at eyebright
Because they are Buddhists of bogs and lakes and mountains
Because they are naked
Because they desire each other like rain and wind
Because they hold their breath, saying, don't let me go
Because they are white islands
Because they are invisible in mist
Because they are mythological
Because they kick and bite
Because they have been to wars
Because they don't take sides
Because they don't care how clever you are
Because they don't care how ignorant you are
Because they are faithful
Because they are grey or white
And from a distance look like clouds.

On Weather

The grass froze to white last night.
This morning there's a skinning wind
Blowing down off the bare back of the hills .

I mentioned the icy frost to Dan's pony,
Molly, but she just looked at me
As if she was thinking to herself:

You'd want to be here in the deep of winter:

You can't open your mouth
      For the wind;
You can't button your coat
      For the rain;
You can't see the hills
      For the mist.

And the worst of it is,

I have to stand here
      On this bleak bog
Like a miserable sentry
      Guarding a wall,
When only a crazed fool
      Would steal a stone.

If I had been thinking,
I wouldn't have brought up
The white frost and skinning wind;

I would have avoided the weather altogether.
And then? What else would I have spoken of
To a Connemara pony on a chilly April morning?

A Winter Sonnet

With a view of Connemara

One man, one woman, solitary, leafless.
Two stone sheds with corrugated roofs.
Three doors made of weathered boards.
Four clouds on the hills imitating trees.

Five heartbroken cottages, nobody home.
Six white shirts dancing in the breeze.
Seven lost blackbirds searching for trees.
Eight scarecrows frightening the air.

Nine currachs sleeping on the rocks.
Ten sheep, the ram dead. Ten gorse widows.
Eleven bare fields planted with weeds.
Twelve gateposts holding nothing in.

Thirteen ponies sheltering, coats like bog cotton.
Fourteen clouds gathering, the storm coming on.

And I could go on like this for hours,
Adding mist to cloud, cloud to rain,
Rain to lake, lake to reeds, reeds to river
To duck, to feather, to bog, to herb, to pony

Until the whole lot collapses in on itself
And looks more and more like Connemara.
That wildness some God forgot to bless,
And so is blest by rain and sun and mist
                              And is the better for it.

The ponies will tell you the story
Of how this came to be.

The Pony's Stare

She turns her gaze on the mountains
Her face all grey like the oncoming rain.

Shelter from the Storms

I was surprised to find an old abandoned car
Sunk into a hollow behind a shelter of rocks.
I thought of Dylan's lines: *We drove that car*
As far as we could, abandoned it out West.
I was singing it still when I came upon Festus
Cutting turf. I mentioned the wrecked car.

"So you have seen my shed, my depot.
What do you make of it? Terrific, what!
I tell you now, there is a grand bit of shelter
In there when a storm comes up out of the hills.

Do you recognise it? It's a Morris Traveller,
A classic. It used belong to my grandfather.
He gave up travelling by pony and trap for that car.
My grandmother hated it: the rattle, the smell, the dust.

They only make the Morris Minor in India now.
But they don't have bogs. Wouldn't you miss a bog?
I hear they think cows are sacred creatures.
I have pulled more cows out of bog holes –

Sacred they may be, but they are certainly dumb.
Now ponies, there's a sacred animal for you.
Sure, when you pass one on the road
You can feel them blessing you with their eyes."

At Maam Cross Pony Show

The old woman said,
"I've always loved ponies.
When I was a girl
I had a pony called Niamh.

I had her about a year,
When one morning, close
To Christmas, she disappeared.

'Abracadabra,' my father said,
Waving his arms about like a magician.
'Poof! Niamh has vanished.
Gone back with Oisín to Tír na nÓg.'

I was heartbroken,
But I believed my father.
It wasn't until I was older,
In an argument with my sister,

I learned that my pony
Had been shot dead
Coming out of bushes –
A hunter had mistaken her for deer.

It was all my fault.
I had tied antlers
To her head for Christmas.
I wanted her to look like Rudolf.

I have never forgiven myself.
It is still a rain that falls
Whenever I see a pony,
Or their hoof prints in the snow."

Stables
With Room Service

Three water buckets
In the yard,
A brush,
A pitchfork,
A shovel
And a wheelbarrow.

In the stables,
Behind a half-door,
A grey stone floor.
After a heavy night
It is covered again
In hay and shite.

And I have the honour to clean it.

Mother to Daughter

A pony will listen to you all day
And grow more and more fond of you
With every kind word you say to her.
They could teach us a thing or two – especially you.

Pony Town

In Connemara there should be a town
Called Pony. There is in Montana.
I went there last year.
Not a futile journey,
You would want to see the prairies
And mountains I crossed. Even in May,
Deep snow lay by the side of the road.

In a bar in Pony, a man who wore a hat indoors
Told me the town was named after a prospector,
Tecumseh Smith, who found gold there in 1866.
He said Tecumseh was a small man, but tough.
He worked out in all weathers so folk called
Him Pony. He was Irish, like you, but named
Tecumseh after the great leader of the Shawnee.

Outside the window were the gas pumps,
The flat bed truck and the sign for cold beer.
The wooden church was higher up the hill,
The old graveyard beyond it. All that was left
Of the gold rush was the dust and a few red brick
Buildings. A one-horse town, I thought, but didn't say it.
"Not a pony in sight," I said.

"That's funny," the man said, "No ponies.
Nobody's ever mentioned that before."
Then he straightened his baseball cap
And went back to cleaning glasses.

Let's Teach Her One Thing at a Time
From a lecture "On Breaking Your Pony", Clifden Pony Show

"First, talk to her softly,
And softer during her breaking.

Keep the movement loose
With her body.

Give her lots of rein,
Don't tie them too short.

That's the way you want her, easy.
You can see right away she's responding.

Breathe easy. Good girl, good girl.
A little saliva in the mouth is fine.

Give her some grass;
It makes her easy.

Brush her tail and her behind,
Watch her along the fence.

It's the first time she'll have things moving
Around where she had nothing move before.

Let her lunge with her mouth open,
Let her know who's in charge.

Go easy with the whip,
Light tap on her bottom will do."

The Will

Festus died last week.
I see in the weekly paper

He left three euro
In his will:

One for his wife,
Two for his pony.

And that's an actual fact;
It's down in black and white.

Now there's a midge-infested lane
You wouldn't want to go down!

Pony and the Sea

He stood in the sea
But it was bigger than a lake,
    Just as it was wider than a river.

He spoke softly to the waves,
But it just murmured a soft Ssseee-Ssseeesss
    Sound he did not understand.

He tried stroking the sea,
But it moved around his legs,
    Hardly noticing he was there.

He tried pissing on the sea,
But it ate his yellow water
    And its smell and its sound.

He tried just being at peace with the sea,
But the wind came up and the waves
    Pushed him back and back.

His hooves dug into the sand,
But the sand shifted beneath him; the sand
    Was with the sea. Both were against him.

So he turned his back on the blue sea.
He walked inland. And wondered for days
    Why sailors spoke of it as a woman.

Pony and Crow

Pony stood under the sheltering tree.
Crow balanced on a branch,
His black feathers cast a shadow
Over the curve of pony's white back
So feather light
He hardly
Felt it at all.
Standing there,
Out of the wind,
Pony finally understood
How Crow could fly;
When he looked at his own shadow
He could see it was dark and heavy,
Weighed down by wet grass and stony soil.

Po-Nee Talks to Greybeard the Sculptor about his Grazing Pony

After the 17th Century, Japanese

Greybeard the sculptor carved
A grazing pony out of elephant ivory.

He said it was like making
A cloud into a tree.

"I'm confused," I said,
"Elephants into ponies,

Clouds into trees.
Where is the common thread?"

"Study the silkworm," he said,
"Then study women's breasts,

Hay, honey, bumble bees
And bowls of red cherries.

Look at grey herons,
Watch the flight of the butterfly.

In the evening listen to old
Women chattering together.

Talk to your sleeping dog.
On rainy days read him poetry.

Monks will tell you where to go.
Poets will delay you.

But a dog asks nothing.
They are more like ponies

Who, as you know, have the memory
Of elephants but are better listeners.

Now you see, the pony taught me
Most about standing silent – watching."

Song of the Pony

Pony would love to have sung of the mountain rivers tumbling,
And of the old wooden fence posts that now hold nothing in.
I am sure you have come upon them high up in the mountains,
Their rusted wire gone but still standing there, a sort of never-the-lessness
That appeals to a pony almost as much as wild grasses and seaweed.
And yes, Pony would love to have sung a hymn to the lakes and the bog,
But Pony has the voice of a horse. So Pony leaves the singing to the wind.
He likes to lie down in a sheltered hollow and listen to the tunes
It sings as it blows in off the Atlantic through the gaps in a stone wall.
Like a contented old man, the wind sings songs his father taught him.
Some call them folk songs. Pony calls them sean-nós.
He likes how hare's tail cotton grass, black bog-rushes, bell heather
And milkwort all bow down as the wind passes over them singing.

The Hunters

Half way there,
they turned the pony round.

The day was soft.
The sky was clear.
He wanted to go on.

But they turned the pony round.

They tugged the reins.
They smacked his hide.
They turned the pony round.

He had done the mountains,
The ledge, the rivers.
He'd come to the edge of the wood.

It was all downhill from here.
He could smell the salt in the air;
He wanted to go on. But still,

They turned the pony round.

He knew from old that the water,
The hay, the sweet rest
Were only a few long fields away.

But I heard their curses through the trees
As they turned the pony round
And made back towards the hills.

All that day I thought of the pony.
Often I think of him still.
Yes, even until now.

Naming the Ponies

Shirt, trousers, braces, boots,
And old Ned is dressed.

Then he crosses the room
And stands by the window

Where, as always, the seven ponies
Are already up and dressed.

He has never
Seen them sleeping.

They are early risers
Like larks and hares.

He knows they miss Ruth:
Her hands, her voice.

She was an early riser too,
Always up before him, with her ponies,

The kettle on the stove,
The tea brewing when he came down.

He doesn't dream much
Since Ruth died.

She had a way with ponies.
They like him because they loved her.

The last things she gave him
Were her names for each of them.

Now, every morning
In mist, rain or sun,

He calls their names
Over the gorse like a prayer.

Cuach na Coille

The writer Tim Robinson is searching for facts
About Cuach na Coille (Cuckoo of the Wood).

He says all he knows about me
Is that I was a beautiful horsewoman

Who lived under the trees in Derryclare Wood.
He fears that nobody living can tell him more.

A beautiful horsewoman – he calls ponies horses –
Who lived amongst the trees in Derryclare Wood.

Sure, what more would he want to know?

The names of the men whose beds I warmed?
The number of children I bore them?

Which wells were sacred to me?
Who were my people?

What were my stories?
Whose songs did I sing?

Was I called cuckoo because
I stole men's hearts and then their ponies?

All these flimsy facts have faded
Away like last year's leaves.

I tell you now, if the great God of the West
Allowed me to call on Tim in his warm snuggle

At the end of Roundstone Pier for one night,
What could I tell him that would add to what he already knows

About me: "A beautiful pony woman who lived in Derryclare Wood."
That is sweet as lark song, a footprint to be proud of. The rest is mist.

On Searching for Connemara Ponies in Finland

for Anthony Johnson

I have been in Finland
For five days now.

Last night I travelled by bus
From Helsinki to Turku.

Still no sign of any ponies.
Tonight I travel north to Oulu.

Somebody told me they have
Spotted hoof prints in the snow

But I am not to get my hopes up,
They might be elk.

I will keep you informed. If things
Work out I'll be home by November.

Hopefully I will have some photographs
Of Connemara ponies moving through the snow,

And maybe a small poem that begins:

> *'The sky is so low here*
> *It gets under your skin,*
>
> *Sews a greyness into your soul.*
> *What would it be like in deep winter?*
>
> *Yesterday, I caught a glimpse*
> *Of white ponies, briefly, ghostly,*
>
> *The way you might glimpse*
> *A flock of snow geese heading south.*
>
> *But so much snow fell last night*
> *It wiped out their hoof prints.'*

The Connemara Totem Pole

In this bare landscape
The pole would have to be cut
From one of the few birch trees
That grow in the sheltered
Valley of Ballynahinch,
Or from some weathered fence posts
Nailed together into a fastness,
Or perhaps from sleepers borrowed
From the old Galway-to-Clifden train line.

I see it now
Standing at the gates
Of Ballynahinch,
A Totem rising
Twenty-seven feet in the air:

At the base
Are carved
Rain symbols
Clouds
Mist
The carving
Scrolls upward
With salmon
To represent
The sea people
And otters
Badgers
Foxes
Kites
Eagles
Deer
And the faces
Of John D'Arcy
And Alexander Nimmo
And then fourteen trout
Swimming
Around fiddles
To represent
The fourteen tribes

Of Connemara
And bodhrans
Flutes
A squeezebox
And a harp
And a banjo
A harmonica
And something
Phallic – an oar
Or an upturned
Currach
Or a hooker
Under full red sail
And breasts
Like blackberries
And a moon
And some stars
And spirals
To represent the sun
And near the top
Two seals and
A dolphin
A seagull
An oystercatcher
A wren
An osprey
A cormorant
A lark
And above them
Leaping up
Into the sky
A Connemara pony.

Here and There

Beyond
Ballynahinch,
Snow
And
Ponies'
Hooves
In
Snow,
And
Ice
On
The
Birch
Trees.

Tony Curtis was born in Dublin in 1955. He studied literature at Essex University and Trinity College Dublin. An award-winning poet, Curtis has published eight warmly received collections. His most recent collections are: *'Folk'* (Arc Publications 2011) and *'An Elephant Called Rex And A Dog Called Dumbo: poems for children'* (with illustrations by Pat Mooney) 2011. Also in that year, *'Sand Works'*, with photographs by Liam Blake, was published. In 2003 he was awarded the Varuna House Exchange Fellowship to Australia. In 2008, *'Days Like These'* (with Paula Meehan and Theo Dorgan) was published by The Brooding Heron Press in Washington State. Curtis has been awarded the Irish National Poetry Prize and has read his poetry all over the world to great acclaim. He is a member of Aosdána.

Note of thanks.

I would like to thank Jim Savage and Dave Lilburn for suggesting the Connemara pony. I would like to lift my hat to Joseph Wilson, Patrick O'Flaherty and everyone at Ballynahinch Castle who helped in the early stages of making the book – when I went out to be with the ponies. Special thanks are due to poets Sally and Samuel Green and Professor Sean McDowell for all their help, suggestions and kind words. Some of these poems first appeared in *'New Hibernia Review'* (St. Paul, Minnesota), *'Tintean'* (Melbourne) and *'Clover'* (Bellingham, Washington State). Thanks are due to all the editors. Finally, I would like to thank the Connemara pony, that most beautiful and mythological of creatures. To all who lift and read this book, my thanks and blessings on you all – ride on.

David Lilburn was born in Limerick in 1950. He studied history at Trinity College Dublin, lithography at L'Istituto d'Arte, Urbino, and art and design at Limerick School of Art and Design. He has won a number of awards and public commissions including the sculptural installation *'A Map'*, for Mary Immaculate College, Limerick 2010/2011; *'In Medias Res'*, a print installation for 'James Joyce and ULYSSES at the National Library of Ireland', Dublin, 2004 and *'Coastline'*, a print installation at the 'Irish Pavillion, Expo 2000, Hanover, Germany. In 2011 he was awarded a Residency at Ballinglen Arts Foundation. Recent exhibitions include *'Voyage: sea journeys, island-hopping & trans-oceanic concepts'*, Künstlerhaus, Dortmund, 2013 and *'Islands'*, Custom House Gallery, Westport, 2012.
In 2009 *'Walking Drawing Making Memory: A Ballynahinch Sketchbook'* was published by Occasional Press in collaboration with Ballynahinch Castle.
www.DavidLilburn.ie

A note on the images

A number of the images in the book were drawn directly in response to Tony's poems. Others derived from sketchbooks I have made over the years in Connemara, sometimes as a welcome guest of Patrick O'Flaherty and Ballynahinch Castle. A number of images were also directly inspired by a wonderful portfolio of photographs by Joe Wilson, an enthusiastic supporter of the project - to him many thanks. Thanks also to Padraig O'Callaghan for his photographs of the Connemara pony.

'Pony'
Poems by Tony Curtis
Images by David Lilburn
First published by Occasional Press
in collaboration with Ballynahinch Castle, 2013
in a limited edition of 130 hardback copies
which include a signed original print
by David Lilburn and Tony Curtis
and 320 paperback copies
Reprint of 500 paperbacks, 2014

Occasional Press, Aghabullogue, County Cork, Ireland
www.occasionalpress.net

Ballynahinch Castle, Recess, Connemara, Co. Galway, Ireland
www.ballynahinch-castle.com

Paperback: ISBN 978-0-9564786-5-8
Hardback: ISBN 978-0-9564786-4-1

Design and Production: David Lilburn, Jim Savage
Photograph of Tony Curtis by Mary Canavan
Photograph of David Lilburn by Eoin Stephenson

Silkscreen printed by Pam Dunne
Typeface Aldine 721
Printed on Hello Matt 170gm^2
by Nicholson & Bass Ltd